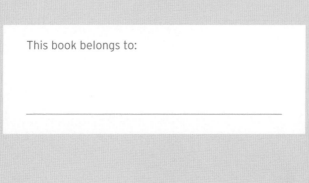

This book belongs to:

_____

TWO MINUTE
MORNINGS

a journal

Neil Pasricha

CHRONICLE BOOKS
SAN FRANCISCO

ISBN 978-1-4521-6346-8

Manufactured in China

Design by Tonje Vetleseter

10 9

Chronicle books and gifts are available at special quantity discounts to corporations, professional associations, literacy programs, and other organizations. For details and discount information, please contact our corporate/premiums department at corporatesales@chroniclebooks.com or at 1-800-759-0190.

Chronicle Books LLC
680 Second Street
San Francisco, California 94107
www.chroniclebooks.com

INTRODUCTION

Life gets busy . . . fast.

Have you ever found yourself with so many browser tabs open you can't see the titles anymore? Or discovered your pockets full with little scrap paper notes you wrote to yourself throughout the day? Or felt anxious about your jammed schedule for tomorrow because you have no time to focus on what matters?

That was a freeze-frame capture of me every day for the past few years.

I was running Leadership Development inside the world's largest company while writing books like *The Happiness Equation* and *The Book of Awesome* to teach people how to find mindfulness.

Yet I couldn't find it myself.

Well, it turns out the solution was right in front of me the whole time.

Based on positive psychology research, I began developing a simple system for myself called Two Minute Mornings.

After I woke up, I spent the first two minutes of my day filling in my answers to three simple sentences:

1   I WILL LET GO OF . . .
2   I AM GRATEFUL FOR . . .
3   I WILL FOCUS ON . . .

The difference in my life was both *immediate* and *incredible*.

The two minutes helped me suddenly "win the morning," which helped start momentum toward me "winning the day."

Letting go of something stressful helped me avoid mentally revisiting a worry throughout the day. The gratitude helped me be more positive every morning. And by deciding what to focus on, I helped align my goals and made sure I was investing in myself.

These two minutes helped make sure I was going the right direction . . . in the right frame of mind.

If you're not already sold, scientific research supports the positive effect of all these actions, too. (More on this in the Why It Works section, following.)

So what is *Two Minute Mornings*?

It's a simple journal to help you rig the game so you can win it. It's a quick therapeutic intervention from our future-focused society to both feel better *and* get more done. No wonder research shows that a positive mindset results in 31 percent higher productivity, 37 percent higher sales, and three times more creativity.

All from taking a few moments to let go of something, feel grateful, and bring some focus to your day.

Two Minute Mornings is by far the best two minutes of my day, every day.

I hope it becomes yours, too.

Neil

WHY IT WORKS

ON LETTING GO

Research reported in *Science* magazine titled "Don't Look Back in Anger!" by Brassen, Gamer, Peters, Gluth, and Büchel (2012) shows that minimizing our regrets as we age creates greater contentment and happiness. The research also shows that holding on to regrets causes us to engage in more aggressive and risky behaviors in the future. The healthiest and happiest people notice mistakes in their lives and then choose to let them go. This written exercise crystallizes that effect and allows those errors in judgment to pass through your mind instead of letting them grate on your mind all day.

ON GRATITUDE

Research by Emmons and McCullough (2003) shows if you write down five gratitudes a week, you're measurably happier over a ten-week period. Research shows the more *specific* you are, the better. We know if people write down "family, food, job" or something similarly vague over and over, it really doesn't cause an increase in happiness. Our minds don't *relive* any specific experience. Try things like "When Trooper learned to shake a paw," "The moment I saw Ana bringing me a coffee," or "How Antonio finally put the toilet seat down," etc.

ON CREATING A DAILY FOCUS

The goal of the daily focus is to strip away the endless list of things you *could do* into a bite-size list of things you *will do*. Why? Because if you don't, you will mentally revisit your *could-do* list all day. And that will cause decision fatigue. See, decision-making energy uses a particularly complex part of the brain, and we're wasting energy anytime we're unfocused. As Florida State Professor of Psychology Roy Baumeister and *New York Times* journalist John Tierney say in *Willpower: Rediscovering the Greatest Human Strength*, "Decision fatigue helps explain why ordinarily sensible people get angry at colleagues and families, splurge on clothes, buy junk food at the supermarket, and can't resist the dealer's offer to rust-proof their new car. No matter how rational and high-minded you try to be, you can't make decision after decision without paying a biological price. It's different from ordinary physical fatigue—you're not consciously aware of being tired—but you're low on mental energy."

I use the daily focus to write down three small goals I want to achieve (and importantly *can achieve*) that day. It feels great crossing them off and satisfying to close the day on a high. If I missed one, I can just add it to tomorrow. An example? "Call Erin about PR campaign, fix bug on website, and do a happiness exercise."

Happiness exercise? Yes! I recommend putting in one a day when you can. They are small proven investments in your positive mindset. Here are the four I use most often:

Exercise: Pennsylvania State University researchers reported in the *Journal of Sport & Exercise Psychology* that the more physically active people are, the greater their feelings of excitement and enthusiasm.

Journaling: A University of Texas study by Slatcher and Pennebaker called "How Do I Love Thee? Let Me Count the Words" showed that people who journaled for three consecutive days improved their communication, the quality of their relationships, and therefore, their happiness.

Meditation: A study by Massachusetts General Hospital shows that a few minutes of silent deep breathing increases activity to your prefrontal cortex, the part of your brain responsible for focus and attention.

Random Kindness: Professor Sonja Lyubomirsky, author of *The How of Happiness*, asked Stanford students to perform five random acts of kindness over a week. Not surprisingly, they reported much higher happiness levels than the control group. Why? They felt good about themselves! People appreciated them. In his book *Flourish*, Professor Martin E. P. Seligman says that "we scientists have found that doing a kindness produces the single most reliable momentary increase in well-being of any exercise we have tested."

Did you do something else that you want to focus on that you know will contribute to your happiness? Maybe jamming on the drums, unplugging your phone all afternoon, deleting a social media app, or finishing a book you love? Write it down!

12/27/19   (night time)   FROM JANAE :)

I WILL LET GO OF . . .

my boards prep & results of how I'll get ~~there~~

I AM GRATEFUL FOR . . .

my family who I love and trust to love
me no matter how many times I fail them.

Friends who are gentle and supportive,
who take time to remind me how much
they love me w/ their words & actions

I WILL FOCUS ON . . .

1 ~~not~~ saying positive things.

2 waking up at a reasonable time over break

3 asking Stephen intentional Qs. about his
walk w/ God, & his journey w/ apps

night time

12 / 28 / 19

I WILL LET GO OF . . .

Worrying whether people remember me — the ones
in my life are enough

I AM GRATEFUL FOR . . .

spontaneous trip to Hyatt SFO w/ stephen on
our way to SF for a date.

Friends to visit in SF & places to explore

mom's cooking - leftover hot pot hr stephen 4/

I WILL FOCUS ON . . . (tomorrow)

1 getting through FMK systemic dz

2 catching up w/ caleb

3 Exercise!!

12 /30 /19   whoops, I'm using this wrong
(night time)

I WILL LET GO OF . . .   I'm so proud of Stephen, God.
You were faithful and you
helped him through the past 1.5 years of
struggling at the LMDT before
I AM GRATEFUL FOR . . .   finally moving to the GRE.
you are so faithful, God.
- Today. I studied @ sue's. steven's class dm
- Dinner w/ Annie & every able to catch up
  with her and meet Luna.
- Took Stephen out to celebrate & we got to
  talk about our goals for 2020.

I WILL FOCUS ON . . . (2020)

1 living mindfully. Taking care of my body is
   worship to the Lord. setting time apart to
   be quiet.

2 _____

3 _____

Writing for twenty minutes about a positive experience
dramatically improves happiness. Your brain relives
it while writing it . . . and while reading it.

1 / 1 / 2020

I WILL LET GO OF . . .

being perfect or pressuring myself

I AM GRATEFUL FOR . . .

- Hard talks, but honest talks w/ Elaine
- Mom's cooking
- a new year and a new decade.
  2010 was when I was a sophomore
  in high school!

  I went through high school,
I WILL FOCUS ON . . .   college, and most of
1 _____ optometry school. I travelled
  to europe twice, asia, twice,
2 _____
  & Jamaica, lived in another
  state ... will finish this —
3 _____
  need new pen.

1 / 7 / 2020

I WILL LET GO OF . . .

trying to be 100% on all the time - it's not
sustainable

I AM GRATEFUL FOR . . .

① a sweet attending in cls
② this hydroflask mug from amnis - ♡ coffee
③ mom preparing food for me.

I WILL FOCUS ON . . .

1 ocular anatomy & 2 videos.

2 exercise - 10 min pushups/situps & run

3 BV chart review

I WILL LET GO OF . . .

_____

I AM GRATEFUL FOR . . .

Jeremiah 33:3
Call to me & I will answer you
and tell you great & unsearchable
things you do not know"

I WILL FOCUS ON . . .

1 _____

2 _____

3 _____

___ /___ /___

I WILL LET GO OF . . .

_____

I AM GRATEFUL FOR . . .

I WILL FOCUS ON . . .

1 _____

2 _____

3 _____

I WILL LET GO OF . . .

_____

I AM GRATEFUL FOR . . .

I WILL FOCUS ON . . .

1 _____

2 _____

3 _____

__ /__ /__

I WILL LET GO OF . . .

_____

I AM GRATEFUL FOR . . .

I WILL FOCUS ON . . .

1 _____

2 _____

3 _____

THREE WALKS

Pennsylvania State University researchers reported in the *Journal of Sport & Exercise Psychology* that the more physically active people are, the greater their general feelings of excitement and enthusiasm. Researcher Amanda Hyde reports, "We found that people who are more physically active have more pleasant-activated feelings than people who are less active, and we also found that people have more pleasant-activated feelings on days when they are more physically active than usual." It doesn't take much: Half an hour of brisk walking three times a week improves happiness. The American Psychosomatic Society published a study showing how Michael Babyak and a team of doctors found that three thirty-minute brisk walks or jogs even improve recovery from clinical depression. Yes, clinical depression. Results were stronger than those from studies using medication or studies using exercise and medication combined.

___ / ___ / ___

I WILL LET GO OF . . .

_____

I AM GRATEFUL FOR . . .

I WILL FOCUS ON . . .

1 _____

2 _____

3 _____

_ / _ / _

I WILL LET GO OF . . .

_____

I AM GRATEFUL FOR . . .

I WILL FOCUS ON . . .

1 _____

2 _____

3 _____

__ /__ /__

I WILL LET GO OF . . .

_____

I AM GRATEFUL FOR . . .

I WILL FOCUS ON . . .

1 _____

2 _____

3 _____

Cultivate your awareness. Embrace your inner
three-year-old. Try to see everything like you're
seeing it for the first time.

I WILL LET GO OF . . .

_____

I AM GRATEFUL FOR . . .

I WILL FOCUS ON . . .

1 _____

2 _____

3 _____

__ /__ /__

I WILL LET GO OF . . .

_____

I AM GRATEFUL FOR . . .

I WILL FOCUS ON . . .

1 _____

2 _____

3 _____

_ / _ / _

I WILL LET GO OF . . .

_____

I AM GRATEFUL FOR . . .

I WILL FOCUS ON . . .

1 _____

2 _____

3 _____

__ /__ /__

I WILL LET GO OF . . .

_____

I AM GRATEFUL FOR . . .

I WILL FOCUS ON . . .

1 _____

2 _____

3 _____

_ /_ /_

I WILL LET GO OF . . .

_____

I AM GRATEFUL FOR . . .

I WILL FOCUS ON . . .

1 _____

2 _____

3 _____

__ /__ /__

I WILL LET GO OF . . .

_____

I AM GRATEFUL FOR . . .

I WILL FOCUS ON . . .

1 _____

2 _____

3 _____

I WILL LET GO OF . . .

_____

I AM GRATEFUL FOR . . .

I WILL FOCUS ON . . .

1 _____

2 _____

3 _____

Four simple words to block all criticism?
Do . . . It . . . For . . . You.

__ /__ /__

I WILL LET GO OF . . .

_____

I AM GRATEFUL FOR . . .

I WILL FOCUS ON . . .

1 _____

2 _____

3 _____

__ /__ /__

I WILL LET GO OF . . .

_____

I AM GRATEFUL FOR . . .

I WILL FOCUS ON . . .

1 _____

2 _____

3 _____

___ /___ /___

I WILL LET GO OF . . .

_____

I AM GRATEFUL FOR .*. .

I WILL FOCUS ON . . .

1 _____

2 _____

3 _____

I WILL LET GO OF . . .

_____

I AM GRATEFUL FOR . . .

I WILL FOCUS ON . . .

1 _____

2 _____

3 _____

__ /__ /__

I WILL LET GO OF . . .

_____

I AM GRATEFUL FOR . . .

I WILL FOCUS ON . . .

1 _____

2 _____

3 _____

___ / ___ / ___

I WILL LET GO OF . . .

_____

I AM GRATEFUL FOR . . .

I WILL FOCUS ON . . .

1 _____

2 _____

3 _____

__ /__ /__

I WILL LET GO OF . . .

_____

I AM GRATEFUL FOR . . .

I WILL FOCUS ON . . .

1 _____

2 _____

3 _____

The average person receives 147 emails
a day and checks their phone every four
minutes. Unplug to recharge.

I WILL LET GO OF . . .

_____

I AM GRATEFUL FOR . . .

I WILL FOCUS ON . . .

1 _____

2 _____

3 _____

___ / ___ / ___

I WILL LET GO OF . . .

_____

I AM GRATEFUL FOR . . .

I WILL FOCUS ON . . .

1 _____

2 _____

3 _____

___ / ___ / ___

I WILL LET GO OF . . .

_____

I AM GRATEFUL FOR . . .

I WILL FOCUS ON . . .

1 _____

2 _____

3 _____

__ / __ / __

I WILL LET GO OF . . .

_____

I AM GRATEFUL FOR . . .

I WILL FOCUS ON . . .

1 _____

2 _____

3 _____

_ / _ / _

I WILL LET GO OF . . .

_____

I AM GRATEFUL FOR . . .

I WILL FOCUS ON . . .

1 _____

2 _____

3 _____

__ /__ /__

I WILL LET GO OF . . .

_____

I AM GRATEFUL FOR . . .

I WILL FOCUS ON . . .

1 _____

2 _____

3 _____

___ /___ /___

I WILL LET GO OF . . .

_____

I AM GRATEFUL FOR . . .

I WILL FOCUS ON . . .

1 _____

2 _____

3 _____

__ /__ /__

I WILL LET GO OF . . .

_____

I AM GRATEFUL FOR . . .

I WILL FOCUS ON . . .

1 _____

2 _____

3 _____

___ / ___ / ___

I WILL LET GO OF . . .

_____

I AM GRATEFUL FOR . . .

I WILL FOCUS ON . . .

1 _____

2 _____

3 _____

__ /__ /__

I WILL LET GO OF . . .

_____

I AM GRATEFUL FOR . . .

I WILL FOCUS ON . . .

1 _____

2 _____

3 _____

It's not: GREAT WORK » BIG SUCCESS » BE HAPPY

It is: BE HAPPY » GREAT WORK » BIG SUCCESS

_ / _ / _

I WILL LET GO OF . . .

_____

I AM GRATEFUL FOR . . .

I WILL FOCUS ON . . .

1 _____

2 _____

3 _____

___ /___ /___

I WILL LET GO OF . . .

_____

I AM GRATEFUL FOR . . .

I WILL FOCUS ON . . .

1 _____

2 _____

3 _____

__ / __ / __

I WILL LET GO OF . . .

_____

I AM GRATEFUL FOR . . .

I WILL FOCUS ON . . .

1 _____

2 _____

3 _____

__ /__ /__

I WILL LET GO OF . . .

_____

I AM GRATEFUL FOR . . .

I WILL FOCUS ON . . .

1 _____

2 _____

3 _____

___ / ___ / ___

I WILL LET GO OF . . .

_____

I AM GRATEFUL FOR . . .

I WILL FOCUS ON . . .

1 _____

2 _____

3 _____

__ /__ /__

I WILL LET GO OF . . .

_____

I AM GRATEFUL FOR . . .

I WILL FOCUS ON . . .

1 _____

2 _____

3 _____

_ / _ / _

I WILL LET GO OF . . .

_____

I AM GRATEFUL FOR . . .

I WILL FOCUS ON . . .

1 _____

2 _____

3 _____

__ /__ /__

I WILL LET GO OF . . .

_____

I AM GRATEFUL FOR . . .

I WILL FOCUS ON . . .

1 _____

2 _____

3 _____

_ /_ /_

I WILL LET GO OF . . .

_____

I AM GRATEFUL FOR . . .

I WILL FOCUS ON . . .

1 _____

2 _____

3 _____

Once in a while it's good to enjoy a completely
unproductive, daydreamy day with a slow smile and
no worries. Your brain needs a rest.

__ /__ /__

I WILL LET GO OF . . .

_____

I AM GRATEFUL FOR . . .

I WILL FOCUS ON . . .

1 _____

2 _____

3 _____

__ / __ / __

I WILL LET GO OF . . .

_____

I AM GRATEFUL FOR . . .

I WILL FOCUS ON . . .

1 _____

2 _____

3 _____

THE INSTANT REPLAY

Writing for a few minutes about a positive experience dramatically improves happiness. Why? Because you actually relive the experience as you're writing it and then relive it every time you read it. Your brain sends you back. In a University of Texas study called "How Do I Love Thee? Let Me Count the Words," researchers Richard Slatcher and James Pennebaker had one member of a couple write about their relationship three times a day. Compared to the control group, the couple was more likely to engage in intimate dialogue afterward, and the relationship was more likely to last.

_ / _ / _

I WILL LET GO OF . . .

_____

I AM GRATEFUL FOR . . .

I WILL FOCUS ON . . .

1 _____

2 _____

3 _____

___ / ___ / ___

I WILL LET GO OF . . .

_____

I AM GRATEFUL FOR . . .

I WILL FOCUS ON . . .

1 _____

2 _____

3 _____

I WILL LET GO OF . . .

_____

I AM GRATEFUL FOR . . .

I WILL FOCUS ON . . .

1 _____

2 _____

3 _____

__ /__ /__

I WILL LET GO OF . . .

_____

I AM GRATEFUL FOR . . .

I WILL FOCUS ON . . .

1 _____

2 _____

3 _____

__ /__ /__

I WILL LET GO OF . . .

_____

I AM GRATEFUL FOR . . .

I WILL FOCUS ON . . .

1 _____

2 _____

3 _____

__ / __ / __

I WILL LET GO OF . . .

_____

I AM GRATEFUL FOR . . .

I WILL FOCUS ON . . .

1 _____

2 _____

3 _____

_ / _ / _

I WILL LET GO OF . . .

_____

I AM GRATEFUL FOR . . .

I WILL FOCUS ON . . .

1 _____

2 _____

3 _____

__ /__ /__

I WILL LET GO OF . . .

_____

I AM GRATEFUL FOR . . .

I WILL FOCUS ON . . .

1 _____

2 _____

3 _____

Your relationship with
yourself is the most important
relationship in your life.

__ / __ / __

I WILL LET GO OF . . .

_____

I AM GRATEFUL FOR . . .

I WILL FOCUS ON . . .

1 _____

2 _____

3 _____

__ /__ /__

I WILL LET GO OF . . .

_____

I AM GRATEFUL FOR . . .

I WILL FOCUS ON . . .

1 _____

2 _____

3 _____

_ / _ / _

I WILL LET GO OF . . .

_____

I AM GRATEFUL FOR . . .

I WILL FOCUS ON . . .

1 _____

2 _____

3 _____

__ / __ / __

I WILL LET GO OF . . .

_____

I AM GRATEFUL FOR . . .

I WILL FOCUS ON . . .

1 _____

2 _____

3 _____

__ /_ /_

I WILL LET GO OF . . .

_____

I AM GRATEFUL FOR . . .

I WILL FOCUS ON . . .

1 _____

2 _____

3 _____

__ /__ /__

I WILL LET GO OF . . .

_____

I AM GRATEFUL FOR . . .

I WILL FOCUS ON . . .

1 _____

2 _____

3 _____

__ / __ / __

I WILL LET GO OF . . .

I AM GRATEFUL FOR . . .

I WILL FOCUS ON . . .

1 _____

2 _____

3 _____

__ /__ /__

I WILL LET GO OF . . .

_____

I AM GRATEFUL FOR . . .

I WILL FOCUS ON . . .

1 _____

2 _____

3 _____

__ / _ / _

I WILL LET GO OF . . .

_____

I AM GRATEFUL FOR . . .

I WILL FOCUS ON . . .

1 _____

2 _____

3 _____

__ / __ / __

I WILL LET GO OF . . .

_____

I AM GRATEFUL FOR . . .

I WILL FOCUS ON . . .

1 _____

2 _____

3 _____

_ / _ / _

I WILL LET GO OF . . .

_____

I AM GRATEFUL FOR . . .

I WILL FOCUS ON . . .

1 _____

2 _____

3 _____

Don't find yourself.
Create yourself.

__ / __ / __

I WILL LET GO OF . . .

_____

I AM GRATEFUL FOR . . .

I WILL FOCUS ON . . .

1 _____

2 _____

3 _____

___ / ___ / ___

I WILL LET GO OF . . .

_____

I AM GRATEFUL FOR . . .

I WILL FOCUS ON . . .

1 _____

2 _____

3 _____

__ /__ /__

I WILL LET GO OF . . .

_____

I AM GRATEFUL FOR . . .

I WILL FOCUS ON . . .

1 _____

2 _____

3 _____

_ /_ /_

I WILL LET GO OF . . .

_____

I AM GRATEFUL FOR . . .

I WILL FOCUS ON . . .

1 _____

2 _____

3 _____

__ /__ /__

I WILL LET GO OF . . .

_____

I AM GRATEFUL FOR . . .

I WILL FOCUS ON . . .

1 _____

2 _____

3 _____

_ / _ / _

I WILL LET GO OF . . .

_____

I AM GRATEFUL FOR . . .

I WILL FOCUS ON . . .

1 _____

2 _____

3 _____

__ /__ /__

I WILL LET GO OF . . .

_____

I AM GRATEFUL FOR . . .

I WILL FOCUS ON . . .

1 _____

2 _____

3 _____

___ /___ /___

I WILL LET GO OF . . .

_____

I AM GRATEFUL FOR . . .

I WILL FOCUS ON . . .

1 _____

2 _____

3 _____

__ / __ / __

I WILL LET GO OF . . .

_____

I AM GRATEFUL FOR . . .

I WILL FOCUS ON . . .

1 _____

2 _____

3 _____

It is easier to act yourself into a new
way of thinking than to think yourself
into a new way of acting.

_ / _ / _

I WILL LET GO OF . . .

_____

I AM GRATEFUL FOR . . .

I WILL FOCUS ON . . .

1 _____

2 _____

3 _____

__ /__ /__

I WILL LET GO OF . . .

_____

I AM GRATEFUL FOR . . .

I WILL FOCUS ON . . .

1 _____

2 _____

3 _____

I WILL LET GO OF . . .

_____

I AM GRATEFUL FOR . . .

I WILL FOCUS ON . . .

1 _____

2 _____

3 _____

___ / ___ / ___

I WILL LET GO OF . . .

_____

I AM GRATEFUL FOR . . .

I WILL FOCUS ON . . .

1 _____

2 _____

3 _____

___ /___ /___

I WILL LET GO OF . . .

_____

I AM GRATEFUL FOR . . .

I WILL FOCUS ON . . .

1 _____

2 _____

3 _____

__ /__ /__

I WILL LET GO OF . . .

I AM GRATEFUL FOR . . .

I WILL FOCUS ON . . .

1 _____

2 _____

3 _____

__ /__ /__

I WILL LET GO OF . . .

_____

I AM GRATEFUL FOR . . .

I WILL FOCUS ON . . .

1 _____

2 _____

3 _____

__ /__ /__

I WILL LET GO OF . . .

_____

I AM GRATEFUL FOR . . .

I WILL FOCUS ON . . .

1 _____

2 _____

3 _____

We can't acquire time. But we
can structure our time so we can
get more out of our lives.

_ / _ / _

I WILL LET GO OF . . .

_____

I AM GRATEFUL FOR . . .

I WILL FOCUS ON . . .

1 _____

2 _____

3 _____

__ /__ /__

I WILL LET GO OF . . .

_____

I AM GRATEFUL FOR . . .

I WILL FOCUS ON . . .

1 _____

2 _____

3 _____

___ / ___ / ___

I WILL LET GO OF . . .

_____

I AM GRATEFUL FOR . . .

I WILL FOCUS ON . . .

1 _____

2 _____

3 _____

__ /__ /__

I WILL LET GO OF . . .

_____

I AM GRATEFUL FOR . . .

I WILL FOCUS ON . . .

1 _____

2 _____

3 _____

__ / __ / __

I WILL LET GO OF . . .

_____

I AM GRATEFUL FOR . . .

I WILL FOCUS ON . . .

1 _____

2 _____

3 _____

__ /__ /__

I WILL LET GO OF . . .

_____

I AM GRATEFUL FOR . . .

I WILL FOCUS ON . . .

1 _____

2 _____

3 _____

I WILL LET GO OF . . .

_____

I AM GRATEFUL FOR . . .

I WILL FOCUS ON . . .

1 _____

2 _____

3 _____

__ / __ / __

I WILL LET GO OF . . .

_____

I AM GRATEFUL FOR . . .

I WILL FOCUS ON . . .

1 _____

2 _____

3 _____

_ / _ / _

I WILL LET GO OF . . .

_____

I AM GRATEFUL FOR . . .

I WILL FOCUS ON . . .

1 _____

2 _____

3 _____

The goal is not to be
perfect. The goal is to
be better than before.

___ / ___ / ___

I WILL LET GO OF . . .

_____

I AM GRATEFUL FOR . . .

I WILL FOCUS ON . . .

1 _____

2 _____

3 _____

_ / _ / _

I WILL LET GO OF . . .

_____

I AM GRATEFUL FOR . . .

I WILL FOCUS ON . . .

1 _____

2 _____

3 _____

___ / ___ / ___

I WILL LET GO OF . . .

_____

I AM GRATEFUL FOR . . .

I WILL FOCUS ON . . .

1 _____

2 _____

3 _____

_ / _ / _

I WILL LET GO OF . . .

_____

I AM GRATEFUL FOR . . .

I WILL FOCUS ON . . .

1 _____

2 _____

3 _____

__ /__ /__

I WILL LET GO OF . . .

_____

I AM GRATEFUL FOR . . .

I WILL FOCUS ON . . .

1 _____

2 _____

3 _____

CONSCIOUS ACTS OF KINDNESS

Carrying out five random acts of kindness a week dramatically improves your happiness. We don't naturally think about paying for a coworker's coffee, chopping veggies for our spouse's lunch, or writing a thank-you note to our apartment building security guard at Christmas. But Sonja Lyubomirsky, author of *The How of Happiness*, did a study asking Stanford students to perform five random acts of kindness over a week. Not surprisingly, they reported much higher happiness levels than the control group. Why? They felt good about themselves! People appreciated them. In his book *Flourish*, Professor Martin Seligman says that "we scientists have found that doing a kindness produces the single most reliable momentary increase in well-being of any exercise we have tested."

__ /__ /__

I WILL LET GO OF . . .

_____

I AM GRATEFUL FOR . . .

I WILL FOCUS ON . . .

1 _____

2 _____

3 _____

_ /_ /_

I WILL LET GO OF . . .

_____

I AM GRATEFUL FOR . . .

I WILL FOCUS ON . . .

1 _____

2 _____

3 _____

__ /__ /__

I WILL LET GO OF . . .

_____

I AM GRATEFUL FOR . . .

I WILL FOCUS ON . . .

1 _____

2 _____

3 _____

_ / _ / _

I WILL LET GO OF . . .

_____

I AM GRATEFUL FOR . . .

I WILL FOCUS ON . . .

1 _____

2 _____

3 _____

__ /__ /__

I WILL LET GO OF . . .

_____

I AM GRATEFUL FOR . . .

I WILL FOCUS ON . . .

1 _____

2 _____

3 _____

Don't choose unhappiness
over uncertainty.

_ / _ / _

I WILL LET GO OF . . .

_____

I AM GRATEFUL FOR . . .

I WILL FOCUS ON . . .

1 _____

2 _____

3 _____

__ /__ /__

I WILL LET GO OF . . .

_____

I AM GRATEFUL FOR . . .

I WILL FOCUS ON . . .

1 _____

2 _____

3 _____

I WILL LET GO OF . . .

_____

I AM GRATEFUL FOR . . .

I WILL FOCUS ON . . .

1 _____

2 _____

3 _____

__ / __ / __

I WILL LET GO OF . . .

_____

I AM GRATEFUL FOR . . .

I WILL FOCUS ON . . .

1 _____

2 _____

3 _____

___ / ___ / ___

I WILL LET GO OF . . .

_____

I AM GRATEFUL FOR . . .

I WILL FOCUS ON . . .

1 _____

2 _____

3 _____

__ /__ /__

I WILL LET GO OF . . .

_____

I AM GRATEFUL FOR . . .

I WILL FOCUS ON . . .

1 _____

2 _____

3 _____

___ /___ /___

I WILL LET GO OF . . .

_____

I AM GRATEFUL FOR . . .

I WILL FOCUS ON . . .

1 _____

2 _____

3 _____

___ /___ /___

I WILL LET GO OF . . .

_____

I AM GRATEFUL FOR . . .

I WILL FOCUS ON . . .

1 _____

2 _____

3 _____

__ /__ /__

I WILL LET GO OF . . .

_____

I AM GRATEFUL FOR . . .

I WILL FOCUS ON . . .

1 _____

2 _____

3 _____

___ /___ /___

I WILL LET GO OF . . .

_____

I AM GRATEFUL FOR . . .

I WILL FOCUS ON . . .

1 _____

2 _____

3 _____

Ten most important
two-letter words: If it is
to be it is up to me.

_ / _ / _

I WILL LET GO OF . . .

_____

I AM GRATEFUL FOR . . .

I WILL FOCUS ON . . .

1 _____

2 _____

3 _____

__ /__ /__

I WILL LET GO OF . . .

_____

I AM GRATEFUL FOR . . .

I WILL FOCUS ON . . .

1 _____

2 _____

3 _____

_ / _ / _

I WILL LET GO OF . . .

_____

I AM GRATEFUL FOR . . .

I WILL FOCUS ON . . .

1 _____

2 _____

3 _____

___ /___ /___

I WILL LET GO OF . . .

_____

I AM GRATEFUL FOR . . .

I WILL FOCUS ON . . .

1 _____

2 _____

3 _____

I WILL LET GO OF . . .

_____

I AM GRATEFUL FOR . . .

I WILL FOCUS ON . . .

1 _____

2 _____

3 _____

__ /__ /__

I WILL LET GO OF . . .

_____

I AM GRATEFUL FOR . . .

I WILL FOCUS ON . . .

1 _____

2 _____

3 _____

___ /___ /___

I WILL LET GO OF . . .

_____

I AM GRATEFUL FOR . . .

I WILL FOCUS ON . . .

1 _____

2 _____

3 _____

___ / ___ / ___

I WILL LET GO OF . . .

_____

I AM GRATEFUL FOR . . .

I WILL FOCUS ON . . .

1 _____

2 _____

3 _____

__ /__ /__

I WILL LET GO OF . . .

I AM GRATEFUL FOR . . .

I WILL FOCUS ON . . .

1

2

3

The deep-down version of you is the best
version of all. You are unique and complicated.
You are different and dimensional.

___ / ___ / ___

I WILL LET GO OF . . .

_____

I AM GRATEFUL FOR . . .

I WILL FOCUS ON . . .

1 _____

2 _____

3 _____

_ / _ / _

I WILL LET GO OF . . .

_____

I AM GRATEFUL FOR . . .

I WILL FOCUS ON . . .

1 _____

2 _____

3 _____

__ /__ /__

I WILL LET GO OF . . .

_____

I AM GRATEFUL FOR . . .

I WILL FOCUS ON . . .

1 _____

2 _____

3 _____

_ / _ / _

I WILL LET GO OF . . .

_____

I AM GRATEFUL FOR . . .

I WILL FOCUS ON . . .

1 _____

2 _____

3 _____

__ /__ /__

I WILL LET GO OF . . .

_____

I AM GRATEFUL FOR . . .

I WILL FOCUS ON . . .

1 _____

2 _____

3 _____

__ /_ /_

I WILL LET GO OF . . .

_____

I AM GRATEFUL FOR . . .

I WILL FOCUS ON . . .

1 _____

2 _____

3 _____

___ /___ /___

I WILL LET GO OF . . .

_____

I AM GRATEFUL FOR . . .

I WILL FOCUS ON . . .

1 _____

2 _____

3 _____

I WILL LET GO OF . . .

_____

I AM GRATEFUL FOR . . .

I WILL FOCUS ON . . .

1 _____

2 _____

3 _____

___ / ___ / ___

I WILL LET GO OF . . .

_____

I AM GRATEFUL FOR . . .

I WILL FOCUS ON . . .

1 _____

2 _____

3 _____

What do you do when you make a mistake?
1 Forgive yourself
2 Move on

_ / _ / _

I WILL LET GO OF . . .

_____

I AM GRATEFUL FOR . . .

I WILL FOCUS ON . . .

1 _____

2 _____

3 _____

__ /__ /__

I WILL LET GO OF . . .

_____

I AM GRATEFUL FOR . . .

I WILL FOCUS ON . . .

1 _____

2 _____

3 _____

I WILL LET GO OF . . .

_____

I AM GRATEFUL FOR . . .

I WILL FOCUS ON . . .

1 _____

2 _____

3 _____

__ /__ /__

I WILL LET GO OF . . .

_____

I AM GRATEFUL FOR . . .

I WILL FOCUS ON . . .

1 _____

2 _____

3 _____

_ /_ /_

I WILL LET GO OF . . .

_____

I AM GRATEFUL FOR . . .

I WILL FOCUS ON . . .

1 _____

2 _____

3 _____

__ /__ /__

I WILL LET GO OF . . .

_____

I AM GRATEFUL FOR . . .

I WILL FOCUS ON . . .

1 _____

2 _____

3 _____

_ / _ / _

I WILL LET GO OF . . .

_____

I AM GRATEFUL FOR . . .

I WILL FOCUS ON . . .

1 _____

2 _____

3 _____

DEEP BREATHING MEDITATIONS

A research team from Massachusetts General
Hospital looked at brain scans of people before
and after they participated in a course on mindfulness meditation and published the results
in *Psychiatry Research*. What happened? After
the course, parts of the brain associated with
compassion and self-awareness grew while parts
associated with stress shrank. Studies report that
meditation can "permanently rewire" your brain
to raise levels of happiness.

_ / _ / _

I WILL LET GO OF . . .

_____

I AM GRATEFUL FOR . . .

I WILL FOCUS ON . . .

1 _____

2 _____

3 _____

__ /__ /__

I WILL LET GO OF . . .

I AM GRATEFUL FOR . . .

I WILL FOCUS ON . . .

1 _____

2 _____

3 _____

_ / _ / _

I WILL LET GO OF . . .

_____

I AM GRATEFUL FOR . . .

I WILL FOCUS ON . . .

1 _____

2 _____

3 _____

__ /__ /__

I WILL LET GO OF . . .

_____

I AM GRATEFUL FOR . . .

I WILL FOCUS ON . . .

1 _____

2 _____

3 _____

According to a Stanford study, 90 percent of our
happiness isn't based on what's happening in the world.
It's based on how we see the world.

_ / _ / _

I WILL LET GO OF . . .

_____

I AM GRATEFUL FOR . . .

I WILL FOCUS ON . . .

1 _____

2 _____

3 _____

__ /__ /__

I WILL LET GO OF . . .

_____

I AM GRATEFUL FOR . . .

I WILL FOCUS ON . . .

1 _____

2 _____

3 _____

_ /_ /_

I WILL LET GO OF . . .

_____

I AM GRATEFUL FOR . . .

I WILL FOCUS ON . . .

1 _____

2 _____

3 _____

__ /__ /__

I WILL LET GO OF . . .

_____

I AM GRATEFUL FOR . . .

I WILL FOCUS ON . . .

1 _____

2 _____

3 _____

_ / _ / _

I WILL LET GO OF . . .

_____

I AM GRATEFUL FOR . . .

I WILL FOCUS ON . . .

1 _____

2 _____

3 _____

__ / __ / __

I WILL LET GO OF . . .

_____

I AM GRATEFUL FOR . . .

I WILL FOCUS ON . . .

1 _____

2 _____

3 _____

_ / _ / _

I WILL LET GO OF . . .

_____

I AM GRATEFUL FOR . . .

I WILL FOCUS ON . . .

1 _____

2 _____

3 _____

__ /__ /__

I WILL LET GO OF . . .

_____

I AM GRATEFUL FOR . . .

I WILL FOCUS ON . . .

1 _____

2 _____

3 _____

_ / _ / _

I WILL LET GO OF . . .

_____

I AM GRATEFUL FOR . . .

I WILL FOCUS ON . . .

1 _____

2 _____

3 _____

___ /___ /___

I WILL LET GO OF . . .

_____

I AM GRATEFUL FOR . . .

I WILL FOCUS ON . . .

1 _____

2 _____

3 _____

_ / _ / _

I WILL LET GO OF . . .

_____

I AM GRATEFUL FOR . . .

I WILL FOCUS ON . . .

1 _____

2 _____

3 _____

Our brains scan the world for problems
and sometimes that's all we see. Happiness is a
choice. And it's hard work.

__ /__ /__

I WILL LET GO OF . . .

_____

I AM GRATEFUL FOR . . .

I WILL FOCUS ON . . .

1 _____

2 _____

3 _____

_ / _ / _

I WILL LET GO OF . . .

_____

I AM GRATEFUL FOR . . .

I WILL FOCUS ON . . .

1 _____

2 _____

3 _____

___ /___ /___

I WILL LET GO OF . . .

_____

I AM GRATEFUL FOR . . .

I WILL FOCUS ON . . .

1 _____

2 _____

3 _____

_ / _ / _

I WILL LET GO OF . . .

_____

I AM GRATEFUL FOR . . .

I WILL FOCUS ON . . .

1 _____

2 _____

3 _____

__ /__ /__

I WILL LET GO OF . . .

_____

I AM GRATEFUL FOR . . .

I WILL FOCUS ON . . .

1 _____

2 _____

3 _____

_ / _ / _

I WILL LET GO OF . . .

_____

I AM GRATEFUL FOR . . .

I WILL FOCUS ON . . .

1 _____

2 _____

3 _____

__ /__ /__

I WILL LET GO OF . . .

_____

I AM GRATEFUL FOR . . .

I WILL FOCUS ON . . .

1 _____

2 _____

3 _____

_ /_ /_

I WILL LET GO OF . . .

_____

I AM GRATEFUL FOR . . .

I WILL FOCUS ON . . .

1 _____

2 _____

3 _____

___ /___ /___

I WILL LET GO OF . . .

_____

I AM GRATEFUL FOR . . .

I WILL FOCUS ON . . .

1 _____

2 _____

3 _____

Don't ask, "What's the first thing
I must do before I can be happy?"
Instead, be happy first.

__ /__ /__

I WILL LET GO OF . . .

_____

I AM GRATEFUL FOR . . .

I WILL FOCUS ON . . .

1 _____

2 _____

3 _____

___ / ___ / ___

I WILL LET GO OF . . .

_____

I AM GRATEFUL FOR . . .

I WILL FOCUS ON . . .

1 _____

2 _____

3 _____

_ /_ /_

I WILL LET GO OF . . .

_____

I AM GRATEFUL FOR . . .

I WILL FOCUS ON . . .

1 _____

2 _____

3 _____

__ / __ / __

I WILL LET GO OF . . .

_____

I AM GRATEFUL FOR . . .

I WILL FOCUS ON . . .

1 _____

2 _____

3 _____

_ /_ /_

I WILL LET GO OF . . .

_____

I AM GRATEFUL FOR . . .

I WILL FOCUS ON . . .

1 _____

2 _____

3 _____

__ /__ /__

I WILL LET GO OF . . .

_____

I AM GRATEFUL FOR . . .

I WILL FOCUS ON . . .

1 _____

2 _____

3 _____

_ / _ / _

I WILL LET GO OF . . .

_____

I AM GRATEFUL FOR . . .

I WILL FOCUS ON . . .

1 _____

2 _____

3 _____

__ /__ /__

I WILL LET GO OF . . .

_____

I AM GRATEFUL FOR . . .

I WILL FOCUS ON . . .

1 _____

2 _____

3 _____

_ / _ / _

I WILL LET GO OF . . .

_____

I AM GRATEFUL FOR . . .

I WILL FOCUS ON . . .

1 _____

2 _____

3 _____

__ /__ /__

I WILL LET GO OF . . .

_____

I AM GRATEFUL FOR . . .

I WILL FOCUS ON . . .

1 _____

2 _____

3 _____

__ /__ /__

I WILL LET GO OF . . .

_____

I AM GRATEFUL FOR . . .

I WILL FOCUS ON . . .

1 _____

2 _____

3 _____

The richest man in the world
can't buy more time. He gets 168 hours
a week just like you and me.

__ /__ /__

I WILL LET GO OF . . .

_____

I AM GRATEFUL FOR . . .

I WILL FOCUS ON . . .

1 _____

2 _____

3 _____

_ / _ / _

I WILL LET GO OF . . .

_____

I AM GRATEFUL FOR . . .

I WILL FOCUS ON . . .

1 _____

2 _____

3 _____

__ /__ /__

I WILL LET GO OF . . .

_____

I AM GRATEFUL FOR . . .

I WILL FOCUS ON . . .

1 _____

2 _____

3 _____

_ / _ / _

I WILL LET GO OF . . .

_____

I AM GRATEFUL FOR . . .

I WILL FOCUS ON . . .

1 _____

2 _____

3 _____

__ /__ /__

I WILL LET GO OF . . .

_____

I AM GRATEFUL FOR . . .

I WILL FOCUS ON . . .

1 _____

2 _____

3 _____

_ / _ / _

I WILL LET GO OF . . .

_____

I AM GRATEFUL FOR . . .

I WILL FOCUS ON . . .

1 _____

2 _____

3 _____

__ /__ /__

I WILL LET GO OF . . .

_____

I AM GRATEFUL FOR . . .

I WILL FOCUS ON . . .

1 _____

2 _____

3 _____

_ / _ / _

I WILL LET GO OF . . .

_____

I AM GRATEFUL FOR . . .

I WILL FOCUS ON . . .

1 _____

2 _____

3 _____

__ /__ /__

I WILL LET GO OF . . .

_____

I AM GRATEFUL FOR . . .

I WILL FOCUS ON . . .

1 _____

2 _____

3 _____

Tip: Add a "yet" to the end
of any sentence you start with
"I can't" or "I don't."

_ / _ / _

I WILL LET GO OF . . .

_____

I AM GRATEFUL FOR . . .

I WILL FOCUS ON . . .

1 _____

2 _____

3 _____

__ /__ /__

I WILL LET GO OF . . .

_____

I AM GRATEFUL FOR . . .

I WILL FOCUS ON . . .

1 _____

2 _____

3 _____

_ / _ / _

I WILL LET GO OF . . .

_____

I AM GRATEFUL FOR . . .

I WILL FOCUS ON . . .

1 _____

2 _____

3 _____

__ /__ /__

I WILL LET GO OF . . .

_____

I AM GRATEFUL FOR . . .

I WILL FOCUS ON . . .

1 _____

2 _____

3 _____

_ / _ / _

I WILL LET GO OF . . .

_____

I AM GRATEFUL FOR . . .

I WILL FOCUS ON . . .

1 _____

2 _____

3 _____

__ /__ /__

I WILL LET GO OF . . .

_____

I AM GRATEFUL FOR . . .

I WILL FOCUS ON . . .

1 _____

2 _____

3 _____

FIVE GRATITUDES

If you can be happy with simple things, then it will be simple to be happy. Some people write in a notebook by their bedside. I wrote five entries a week on my website, 1000awesomethings.com. Back in 2003, researchers Robert Emmons and Michael McCullough asked groups of students to write down five gratitudes, five hassles, or five events that happened over the past week for ten straight weeks. Guess what happened? The students who wrote five gratitudes were happier and physically healthier. Charles Dickens puts this well: "Reflect upon your present blessings, of which every man has many, not your past misfortunes, of which all men have some."

__ / __ / __

I WILL LET GO OF . . .

_____

I AM GRATEFUL FOR . . .

I WILL FOCUS ON . . .

1 _____

2 _____

3 _____

_ / _ / _

I WILL LET GO OF . . .

_____

I AM GRATEFUL FOR . . .

I WILL FOCUS ON . . .

1 _____

2 _____

3 _____

__ /__ /__

I WILL LET GO OF . . .

_____

I AM GRATEFUL FOR . . .

I WILL FOCUS ON . . .

1 _____

2 _____

3 _____

Hitting a wall? Go outside. Your
brain responds differently to different
colors, smells, and sounds.

_ / _ / _

I WILL LET GO OF . . .

_____

I AM GRATEFUL FOR . . .

I WILL FOCUS ON . . .

1 _____

2 _____

3 _____

__ /__ /__

I WILL LET GO OF . . .

_____

I AM GRATEFUL FOR . . .

I WILL FOCUS ON . . .

1 _____

2 _____

3 _____

_ /_ /_

I WILL LET GO OF . . .

_____

I AM GRATEFUL FOR . . .

I WILL FOCUS ON . . .

1 _____

2 _____

3 _____

__ /__ /__

I WILL LET GO OF . . .

_____

I AM GRATEFUL FOR . . .

I WILL FOCUS ON . . .

1 _____

2 _____

3 _____

_ / _ / _

I WILL LET GO OF . . .

_____

I AM GRATEFUL FOR . . .

I WILL FOCUS ON . . .

1 _____

2 _____

3 _____

__ /__ /__

I WILL LET GO OF . . .

_____

I AM GRATEFUL FOR . . .

I WILL FOCUS ON . . .

1 _____

2 _____

3 _____

_ /_ /_

I WILL LET GO OF . . .

_____

I AM GRATEFUL FOR . . .

I WILL FOCUS ON . . .

1 _____

2 _____

3 _____

Every single person gets stuck focusing
on the negative sometimes. It means you're
normal. Fighting it can prolong it.

__ /__ /__

I WILL LET GO OF . . .

_____

I AM GRATEFUL FOR . . .

I WILL FOCUS ON . . .

1 _____

2 _____

3 _____

_ / _ / _

I WILL LET GO OF . . .

_____

I AM GRATEFUL FOR . . .

I WILL FOCUS ON . . .

1 _____

2 _____

3 _____

___ / ___ / ___

I WILL LET GO OF . . .

_____

I AM GRATEFUL FOR . . .

I WILL FOCUS ON . . .

1 _____

2 _____

3 _____

I WILL LET GO OF . . .

_____

I AM GRATEFUL FOR . . .

I WILL FOCUS ON . . .

1 _____

2 _____

3 _____

__ /__ /__

I WILL LET GO OF . . .

_____

I AM GRATEFUL FOR . . .

I WILL FOCUS ON . . .

1 _____

2 _____

3 _____

I WILL LET GO OF . . .

_____

I AM GRATEFUL FOR . . .

I WILL FOCUS ON . . .

1 _____

2 _____

3 _____

__ / __ / __

I WILL LET GO OF . . .

_____

I AM GRATEFUL FOR . . .

I WILL FOCUS ON . . .

1 _____

2 _____

3 _____

Any cliché, quote, or piece of advice that
resonates with you only confirms to your mind
something you already know.

_ / _ / _

I WILL LET GO OF . . .

_____

I AM GRATEFUL FOR . . .

I WILL FOCUS ON . . .

1 _____

2 _____

3 _____

__ / __ / __

I WILL LET GO OF . . .

_____

I AM GRATEFUL FOR . . .

I WILL FOCUS ON . . .

1 _____

2 _____

3 _____

___ / ___ / ___

I WILL LET GO OF . . .

_____

I AM GRATEFUL FOR . . .

I WILL FOCUS ON . . .

1 _____

2 _____

3 _____

___ / ___ / ___

I WILL LET GO OF . . .

_____

I AM GRATEFUL FOR . . .

I WILL FOCUS ON . . .

1 _____

2 _____

3 _____

_ / _ / _

I WILL LET GO OF . . .

I AM GRATEFUL FOR . . .

I WILL FOCUS ON . . .

1 _____

2 _____

3 _____

___ /___ /___

___

I WILL LET GO OF . . .

_____

I AM GRATEFUL FOR . . .

I WILL FOCUS ON . . .

1 _____

2 _____

3 _____

_ / _ / _

I WILL LET GO OF . . .

_____

I AM GRATEFUL FOR . . .

I WILL FOCUS ON . . .

1 _____

2 _____

3 _____

__ /__ /__

I WILL LET GO OF . . .

_____

I AM GRATEFUL FOR . . .

I WILL FOCUS ON . . .

1 _____

2 _____

3 _____

_ / _ / _

I WILL LET GO OF . . .

_____

I AM GRATEFUL FOR . . .

I WILL FOCUS ON . . .

1 _____

2 _____

3 _____

__ /__ /__

I WILL LET GO OF . . .

_____

I AM GRATEFUL FOR . . .

I WILL FOCUS ON . . .

1 _____

2 _____

3 _____

Happy people don't have the best
of everything. They make the best of
everything. Be happy first.

_ / _ / _

I WILL LET GO OF . . .

_____

I AM GRATEFUL FOR . . .

I WILL FOCUS ON . . .

1 _____

2 _____

3 _____

__ /__ /__

I WILL LET GO OF . . .

_____

I AM GRATEFUL FOR . . .

I WILL FOCUS ON . . .

1 _____

2 _____

3 _____

__ / _ / _

I WILL LET GO OF . . .

_____

I AM GRATEFUL FOR . . .

I WILL FOCUS ON . . .

1 _____

2 _____

3 _____

__ /__ /__

I WILL LET GO OF . . .

_____

I AM GRATEFUL FOR . . .

I WILL FOCUS ON . . .

1 _____

2 _____

3 _____

__ /__ /__

I WILL LET GO OF . . .

_____

I AM GRATEFUL FOR . . .

I WILL FOCUS ON . . .

1 _____

2 _____

3 _____

__ /__ /__

I WILL LET GO OF . . .

_____

I AM GRATEFUL FOR . . .

I WILL FOCUS ON . . .

1 _____

2 _____

3 _____

_ / _ / _

I WILL LET GO OF . . .

_____

I AM GRATEFUL FOR . . .

I WILL FOCUS ON . . .

1 _____

2 _____

3 _____

__ /__ /__

I WILL LET GO OF . . .

_____

I AM GRATEFUL FOR . . .

I WILL FOCUS ON . . .

1 _____

2 _____

3 _____

I WILL LET GO OF . . .

_____

I AM GRATEFUL FOR . . .

I WILL FOCUS ON . . .

1 _____

2 _____

3 _____

Know what you're spending
your free time on. And make sure
it's something you love.

__ /__ /__

I WILL LET GO OF . . .

_____

I AM GRATEFUL FOR . . .

I WILL FOCUS ON . . .

1 _____

2 _____

3 _____

_ /_ /_

I WILL LET GO OF . . .

_____

I AM GRATEFUL FOR . . .

I WILL FOCUS ON . . .

1 _____

2 _____

3 _____

__ /__ /__

I WILL LET GO OF . . .

_____

I AM GRATEFUL FOR . . .

I WILL FOCUS ON . . .

1 _____

2 _____

3 _____

_ / _ / _

I WILL LET GO OF . . .

_____

I AM GRATEFUL FOR . . .

I WILL FOCUS ON . . .

1 _____

2 _____

3 _____

__ /__ /__

I WILL LET GO OF . . .

_____

I AM GRATEFUL FOR . . .

I WILL FOCUS ON . . .

1 _____

2 _____

3 _____

__ / __ / __

I WILL LET GO OF . . .

_____

I AM GRATEFUL FOR . . .

I WILL FOCUS ON . . .

1 _____

2 _____

3 _____

__ /__ /__

I WILL LET GO OF . . .

_____

I AM GRATEFUL FOR . . .

I WILL FOCUS ON . . .

1 _____

2 _____

3 _____

_ / _ / _

I WILL LET GO OF . . .

_____

I AM GRATEFUL FOR . . .

I WILL FOCUS ON . . .

1 _____

2 _____

3 _____

__ /__ /__

I WILL LET GO OF . . .

_____

I AM GRATEFUL FOR . . .

I WILL FOCUS ON . . .

1 _____

2 _____

3 _____

If it's not easy,
you're doing it right.

___ / ___ / ___

I WILL LET GO OF . . .

_____

I AM GRATEFUL FOR . . .

I WILL FOCUS ON . . .

1 _____

2 _____

3 _____

__ /__ /__

I WILL LET GO OF . . .

_____

I AM GRATEFUL FOR . . .

I WILL FOCUS ON . . .

1 _____

2 _____

3 _____

_ /_ /_

I WILL LET GO OF . . .

_____

I AM GRATEFUL FOR . . .

I WILL FOCUS ON . . .

1 _____

2 _____

3 _____

__ /__ /__

I WILL LET GO OF . . .

_____

I AM GRATEFUL FOR . . .

I WILL FOCUS ON . . .

1 _____

2 _____

3 _____

_ / _ / _

I WILL LET GO OF . . .

_____

I AM GRATEFUL FOR . . .

I WILL FOCUS ON . . .

1 _____

2 _____

3 _____

__ /__ /__

I WILL LET GO OF . . .

_____

I AM GRATEFUL FOR . . .

I WILL FOCUS ON . . .

1 _____

2 _____

3 _____

__ /__ /__

I WILL LET GO OF . . .

_____

I AM GRATEFUL FOR . . .

I WILL FOCUS ON . . .

1 _____

2 _____

3 _____

__ /__ /__

I WILL LET GO OF . . .

_____

I AM GRATEFUL FOR . . .

I WILL FOCUS ON . . .

1 _____

2 _____

3 _____

Turn your phone off after dinner.
Downtime after work helps us recharge
for the next day.

__ / __ / __

I WILL LET GO OF . . .

_____

I AM GRATEFUL FOR . . .

I WILL FOCUS ON . . .

1 _____

2 _____

3 _____

___ / ___ / ___

I WILL LET GO OF . . .

_____

I AM GRATEFUL FOR . . .

I WILL FOCUS ON . . .

1 _____

2 _____

3 _____

_ /_ /_

I WILL LET GO OF . . .

_____

I AM GRATEFUL FOR . . .

I WILL FOCUS ON . . .

1 _____

2 _____

3 _____

___ / ___ / ___

I WILL LET GO OF . . .

_____

I AM GRATEFUL FOR . . .

I WILL FOCUS ON . . .

1 _____

2 _____

3 _____

_ /_ /_

I WILL LET GO OF . . .

_____

I AM GRATEFUL FOR . . .

I WILL FOCUS ON . . .

1 _____

2 _____

3 _____

A COMPLETE UNPLUG

"The richest, happiest, and most productive lives are characterized by the ability to fully engage in the challenge at hand, but also to disengage periodically and seek renewal," say Jim Loehr and Tony Schwartz in *The Power of Full Engagement*. And a Kansas State University study found that complete downtime after work helps us recharge for the next day. How do you do this in practice? Develop a home for your cell phone that is far away from your bed. My wife and I keep ours on airplane mode in the basement. Also, sometimes I ask her to hide my phone on weekends. Or I leave my work phone in my car in my garage. It's accessible! But the walk to the garage prevents me from incessantly checking it when I don't need to—like just before bed. Some additional measures could be using an Internet parental control app or a time-management solution. These help monitor and control Internet behavior to prevent you from dreaded social media rabbit holes.

_ /_ /_

I WILL LET GO OF . . .

_____

I AM GRATEFUL FOR . . .

I WILL FOCUS ON . . .

1 _____

2 _____

3 _____

__ /__ /__

I WILL LET GO OF . . .

_____

I AM GRATEFUL FOR . . .

I WILL FOCUS ON . . .

1 _____

2 _____

3 _____

_ / _ / _

I WILL LET GO OF . . .

_____

I AM GRATEFUL FOR . . .

I WILL FOCUS ON . . .

1 _____

2 _____

3 _____

__ /__ /__

I WILL LET GO OF . . .

_____

I AM GRATEFUL FOR . . .

I WILL FOCUS ON . . .

1 _____

2 _____

3 _____

_ / _ / _

I WILL LET GO OF . . .

_____

I AM GRATEFUL FOR . . .

I WILL FOCUS ON . . .

1 _____

2 _____

3 _____

If you can be happy with
simple things, then it will be
simple to be happy.

__ /__ /__

I WILL LET GO OF . . .

_____

I AM GRATEFUL FOR . . .

I WILL FOCUS ON . . .

1 _____

2 _____

3 _____

I WILL LET GO OF . . .

_____

I AM GRATEFUL FOR . . .

I WILL FOCUS ON . . .

1 _____

2 _____

3 _____

___ /___ /___

I WILL LET GO OF . . .

_____

I AM GRATEFUL FOR . . .

I WILL FOCUS ON . . .

1 _____

2 _____

3 _____

___ / ___ / ___

I WILL LET GO OF . . .

_____

I AM GRATEFUL FOR . . .

I WILL FOCUS ON . . .

1 _____

2 _____

3 _____

__ / __ / __

I WILL LET GO OF . . .

_____

I AM GRATEFUL FOR . . .

I WILL FOCUS ON . . .

1 _____

2 _____

3 _____

__ /__ /__

I WILL LET GO OF . . .

_____

I AM GRATEFUL FOR . . .

I WILL FOCUS ON . . .

1 _____

2 _____

3 _____

__ /__ /__

I WILL LET GO OF . . .

_____

I AM GRATEFUL FOR . . .

I WILL FOCUS ON . . .

1 _____

2 _____

3 _____

Where do good ideas
come from? The three *B*'s:
Bed, Bathtub, and Bus.

_ / _ / _

I WILL LET GO OF . . .

_____

I AM GRATEFUL FOR . . .

I WILL FOCUS ON . . .

1 _____

2 _____

3 _____

__ / __ / __

I WILL LET GO OF . . .

_____

I AM GRATEFUL FOR . . .

I WILL FOCUS ON . . .

1 _____

2 _____

3 _____

__ / __ / __

I WILL LET GO OF . . .

_____

I AM GRATEFUL FOR . . .

I WILL FOCUS ON . . .

1 _____

2 _____

3 _____

__ /__ /__

I WILL LET GO OF . . .

_____

I AM GRATEFUL FOR . . .

I WILL FOCUS ON . . .

1 _____

2 _____

3 _____

_ / _ / _

I WILL LET GO OF . . .

_____

I AM GRATEFUL FOR . . .

I WILL FOCUS ON . . .

1 _____

2 _____

3 _____

___ /___ /___

I WILL LET GO OF . . .

_____

I AM GRATEFUL FOR . . .

I WILL FOCUS ON . . .

1 _____

2 _____

3 _____

_ / _ / _

I WILL LET GO OF . . .

_____

I AM GRATEFUL FOR . . .

I WILL FOCUS ON . . .

1 _____

2 _____

3 _____

__ /__ /__

I WILL LET GO OF . . .

_____

I AM GRATEFUL FOR . . .

I WILL FOCUS ON . . .

1 _____

2 _____

3 _____

_ / _ / _

I WILL LET GO OF . . .

_____

I AM GRATEFUL FOR . . .

I WILL FOCUS ON . . .

1 _____

2 _____

3 _____

__ /__ /__

I WILL LET GO OF . . .

_____

I AM GRATEFUL FOR . . .

I WILL FOCUS ON . . .

1 _____

2 _____

3 _____

Now is better than later.
Done is better than perfect.
Keep moving.

_ / _ / _

I WILL LET GO OF . . .

_____

I AM GRATEFUL FOR . . .

I WILL FOCUS ON . . .

1 _____

2 _____

3 _____

__ /__ /__

I WILL LET GO OF . . .

_____

I AM GRATEFUL FOR . . .

I WILL FOCUS ON . . .

1 _____

2 _____

3 _____

___ /___ /___

I WILL LET GO OF . . .

_____

I AM GRATEFUL FOR . . .

I WILL FOCUS ON . . .

1 _____

2 _____

3 _____

___ / ___ / ___

I WILL LET GO OF . . .

_____

I AM GRATEFUL FOR . . .

I WILL FOCUS ON . . .

1 _____

2 _____

3 _____

_ /_ /_

I WILL LET GO OF . . .

_____

I AM GRATEFUL FOR . . .

I WILL FOCUS ON . . .

1 _____

2 _____

3 _____

__ /__ /__

I WILL LET GO OF . . .

_____

I AM GRATEFUL FOR . . .

I WILL FOCUS ON . . .

1 _____

2 _____

3 _____

I WILL LET GO OF . . .

_____

I AM GRATEFUL FOR . . .

I WILL FOCUS ON . . .

1 _____

2 _____

3 _____

__ /__ /__

I WILL LET GO OF . . .

_____

I AM GRATEFUL FOR . . .

I WILL FOCUS ON . . .

1 _____

2 _____

3 _____

Want to be happy in twenty minutes?
1 Write a thank-you email: five mins
2 Write down five gratitudes: five mins
3 Go on a run: ten mins

___ / ___ / ___

I WILL LET GO OF . . .

_____

I AM GRATEFUL FOR . . .

I WILL FOCUS ON . . .

1 _____

2 _____

3 _____

___ /___ /___

I WILL LET GO OF . . .

_____

I AM GRATEFUL FOR . . .

I WILL FOCUS ON . . .

1 _____

2 _____

3 _____

_ / _ / _

I WILL LET GO OF . . .

_____

I AM GRATEFUL FOR . . .

I WILL FOCUS ON . . .

1 _____

2 _____

3 _____

___ /___ /___

I WILL LET GO OF . . .

_____

I AM GRATEFUL FOR . . .

I WILL FOCUS ON . . .

1 _____

2 _____

3 _____